ALBERT EINSTEIN

by

PETER N. HAMILTON

LUTTERWORTH PRESS

GUILDFORD AND LONDON

First published 1973
by the Lutterworth Press, Luke House, Guildford, Surrey.

American edition published by the Judson Press, Valley Forge,
Pennsylvania

For

SOPHIE, KATE and LUCY

ISBN 0 7188 1866 0

Printed in Great Britain
at the St. Ann's Press, Park Road, Altrincham Cheshire, WA14 5QQ

**Books are to be returned on or before
the last date below**

MAKERS OF MODERN THOUGHT

EDITOR:

THE REV. DR. A. D. GALLOWAY

PROFESSOR OF DIVINITY, UNIVERSITY OF GLASGOW

CONSULTANT EDITORS: The Rev. Joseph D. Ban (Chaplain, Linfield College, McMinnville, Oregon, U.S.A.), the Rev. Alec Gilmore (Associate Editor, Lutterworth Press), and the Rev. Frank Hoadley (Editor, Judson Press, U.S.A.)

CONTENTS

PREFACE

THIS BOOK is neither a biography of Einstein nor yet another popular book on relativity. Its aim is to describe Einstein's thought on relativity and other problems, including the fascinating way in which he searched for and found inter-relationships between apparently unconnected physical concepts, and to discuss the importance of his work both for science and—because of its fundamental nature—for philosophy. His field is theoretical physics, and his work is all the more interesting to the non-specialist in that it was done not in elaborate laboratories but at a desk, using only paper and pencil and his immense capacity for concentrated thought.

The general reader for whom this book is written could be slightly dismayed by the fact that it contains some algebra, namely, a few straightforward equations. May I reassure him that, whereas Einstein's own work employs very advanced mathematics, this book uses nothing that cannot easily be followed, with a little thought now and again, by someone who gave up mathematics, possibly with a sigh of relief, around the age of fifteen. I say this with confidence: it is part of my job to teach school mathematics at various levels. But, since a number of people shy away from even simple algebra, I have written in such a way that the reader will lose as little as possible if he 'skips' the equations. Selective use of a little algebra does, however, offer most readers a better insight into Einstein's work and ways of thinking than they could otherwise get—an equation is sometimes the simplest way of expressing what would be verbose, and far from clear, if described entirely in words.

Brighton College, Sussex.

P.N.H.

1

LIFE

ALBERT EINSTEIN was born in Ulm in Southern Germany on March 14, 1879, the elder child of Jewish parents who soon moved to Munich, where Albert's father and uncle ran a small factory. His father was an ineffectual man. The main influences upon young Albert came from his uncle, a trained engineer who lived with them, and his mother, from whom he acquired a lifelong love of music. He soon developed a keen sense of wonder at the world around him : at the age of about five he was given a magnetic compass, and as an old man he vividly recalled the awe with which he had watched its needle mysteriously pointing always in the same direction.

At school, Albert disliked the mechanical learning of Latin and Greek; at home, he greatly enjoyed working out his own solutions to simple problems of algebra, in preference to those in a textbook his uncle had given him. Thus began a division between formal work and intellectual pursuits which continued for twenty years. When about thirteen he began eagerly devouring a series of popular books on science. These books also influenced his religious outlook. Young Albert had possessed strong religious feelings and had been attracted to Judaism. But his science books gave a logical account of the world, and of the evolution of life. He came to distrust both Genesis and stories of miracles, and he abandoned traditional religion. But he continued greatly to value its ethical teaching; and throughout his life he held to a firm belief in the harmony and essential simplicity of nature.

When he was fifteen the family business foundered and they moved to Milan, where financial troubles recurred. Albert remained behind at his school, but was lonely, loathed the thought of conscription into the German army, and soon joined his family. Precariously financed by relatives, he then resumed his studies in Switzerland, gaining admission to Zürich Polytechnic in 1896. He was now clear that theoretical physics was his great interest. Disliking formal teaching, he 'cut' many of the lectures. In particular, apart from the lectures of the great mathematician Hermann Minkowski, he largely neglected mathematics. Fortunately, two friends and fellow-students were mathematicians: Marcel Grossman, who quickly recognized Einstein's genius, took assiduous lecture notes, and coached his friend at weekends, together with a Serbian girl student, Mileva Maric, with whom Einstein fell in love.

When Einstein graduated in 1900 his teachers did not select him for a junior post. Work was hard to find. After a series of temporary jobs he was employed in 1902 as an examiner in the Swiss Patent Office in Berne. He developed an interest in gadgetry and enjoyed the work, but his main energies were devoted to working at home, often late into the night, on theoretical physics. His salary now enabled him to marry Mileva. Their marriage seems to have been happy enough at first; Albert was fond of their two sons. But within a few years tensions increased, and the marriage broke up. In 1919, aged forty, he married his widowed and slightly older cousin Elsa, who had nursed him through a major illness. This marriage lasted until her death.

It is clear that physics far outweighed all domestic matters as the dominant interest in Einstein's life. Also he had a very definite scale of values, and saw his work as far more important than his personal life. Once tensions developed in his first marriage it was likely that Einstein would opt for separation.

From 1900 onwards, the dominant feature of Einstein's life was his unrelenting work at some of the deepest problems of physics and mainly, in succession, at three fundamental problems. He solved two, but not the third. The first concerned the nature and propagation of light. Einstein had come to suspect that, whatever the speed of either the light source or the observer, the speed of light never varies. From 1902–5 he wrestled with the problem of interpreting or amending the basic laws of physics to make them compatible with this suspicion. He relieved his mental pressure by solving other problems, but returned again and again to this central problem. Finally, the solution came in a flash of inspiration in 1905. Getting it on paper in logical and mathematical form took five weeks. Relativity was born—and Einstein retired to bed for a fortnight.

Recognition came only slowly. While still at the Patent Office, Einstein began tackling his second fundamental problem, gravitation. His 1905 theory of relativity was 'special' in that its scope deliberately excluded acceleration and gravitation. He now sought out a 'general theory' to include these. This proved an immense task. Einstein's main flash of insight here came in 1907, but its logical and mathematical formulation posed intractable problems and took eight years. This work ranks among man's greatest intellectual feats, even though it is not yet certain whether the precise form of Einstein's solution is correct. Eight years concentrating on a single problem is a very long time, especially when these include personal and international upheavals.

Einstein obtained university posts at Zürich (1909) and Prague (1910); he returned to Zürich Polytechnic in 1912, as professor of theoretical physics. In 1913 he was offered the great honour of membership of the Prussian Academy of Sciences. This carried with it the privilege of lecturing only when he wished : he would be entirely free to do his own work, among some of the greatest intellects in Europe. But he would have to live in Berlin, and membership of the Academy normally carried with it German citizenship. Mileva loved Zürich, and urged him to decline. But Einstein needed this freedom from university commitments. He accepted, on one condition : remembering his detestation of Prussian militarism, he insisted on retaining his Swiss nationality. Einstein went to Berlin alone, his marriage virtually at an end. Mileva and the boys joined him in April, 1914; they disliked Berlin, returned to Zürich for the school holidays, and stayed when war broke out.

The war casualties, and the rampant nationalism pervading even the Academy, appalled Einstein. He joined various small anti-war groups, but soon decided the task was hopeless. Indeed, the war interfered remarkably little with Einstein's concentration, and in 1915 he solved the problem of gravitation with his general theory of relativity.

Dramatic support for this theory came in 1919, when Britain's Astronomer Royal publicly announced that observations made during an eclipse confirmed that on passing near the sun starlight bends, due to the sun's gravitation, through the small angle Einstein had predicted. This bending of light, coupled with *British* confirmation of a theory evolved in wartime *Berlin,* caught the public's imagination.

Having rapidly become world famous, Einstein was not willing wholly to subordinate the needs of mankind to his physics, as he had earlier subordinated domestic matters. He played a prominent part in many efforts to promote peace, and to help Jewish causes. Einstein at times found being a celebrity irksome, but he enjoyed travelling to many countries and speaking to large audiences, who often found his enthusiasm infectious. He once responded to prolonged applause by playing his violin, which happened to be off-stage, as an encore.

From about 1923 Einstein began to concentrate upon his third fundamental problem, the search for a 'unified field theory' whose scope would include electromagnetism and the movements of individual particles, as well as everything covered by his 'general theory'. Most physicists regard this work as a blind alley. Perhaps they are right. Perhaps Einstein's genius was burning out. Or perhaps—as is discussed below—the time was not yet ripe for such a theory, on which however Einstein worked for the rest of his life.

Einstein, as a prominent Jew, was fortunate in being outside Germany when Hitler came to power. He resigned from the Academy and went to America, settling permanently in Princeton, where Elsa died in 1936. Three years later, the file of papers which led President Roosevelt to initiate production of the atomic bomb included a letter from Einstein—the physicist whose work on relativity had, as we shall see, first suggested the theoretical possibility of such explosions. Laboratory work in Berlin and elsewhere indicated that this possibility was very real, and Einstein and others believed that Germany would produce atomic bombs. Reluctantly, Einstein agreed to use his prestige in writing to the President. When America and not Germany used the bomb, Einstein wished he had not written that letter, although he still felt that at the time he had acted rightly. He then made a series of strong appeals for a world government, to which the great powers would pledge all their military might.

Einstein officially retired in 1945, but continued to work—mainly at physics, but also for peace. He declined the offer of the presidency of Israel on the President's death in 1952. His health further deteriorated in 1954, and he died in Princeton on April 18, 1955.

2

THOUGHT

Einstein's Early Work

As a student, Einstein was much interested in recent work on thermodynamics. Boltzmann and others had propounded the kinetic theory of heat, which attributes the pressure a gas exerts to the energy with which its molecules collide with its container, and had developed statistical laws giving the velocity-distribution of large numbers of molecules. In 1902–5, Einstein published several papers on this topic. Then, in 1905, he showed his genius for theoretical physics by applying this theory to liquids, having searched in his mind for a *visible* phenomenon that would confirm the molecular structure of matter—which some scientists still doubted. He assumed that a liquid's molecules would buzz around with a similar velocity-distribution-pattern to those of a gas: this enabled him to calculate the precise type of zigzag path in which a long, thin particle suspended on the surface of a liquid would be pushed around as molecules bump into it. He did not know that a naturalist, Robert Brown, had observed (but not explained) this 'Brownian notion' with his microscope 80 years earlier. Einstein's detailed calculations were later confirmed experimentally by J. Perrin.

For many years the principal controversy in physics had concerned the nature and propagation of light.

Newton's suggestion that light may consist of streams of tiny particles or corpuscles was now generally rejected in favour of the *wave theory* of light propounded by Newton's contemporary, Huygens. Newton's explanation of the familiar 'refraction' or bending of light as it passes from water to air required that light must travel *faster* in water: experiments had shown that it travels *slower*. Also 'diffraction', the phenomenon that after passing through a small hole a light ray spreads out into concentric rings of light and shadow, indicates that this light spreads out *like a wave*. The wave theory of light also gained support from Maxwell's important work on electricity and magnetism. In developing the key concept of a *field of force*—best known in the case of the field-lines along which iron filings arrange themselves near a magnet—Maxwell had obtained the general set of equations from which any particular electrical or magnetic field can be calculated; for the simple case of a vibrating electric charge these equations are the standard equations for a *wave* moving with constant velocity, namely *the velocity of light*. This suggests a kinship between light and electromagnetic wave-radiation.

But the wave theory of light faced a formidable objection. It was assumed that waves can only travel through a medium: Huygens had postulated an invisible, all-pervading 'ether' as such a medium. Now an ether filling all space is presumably stationary, so that in orbiting the sun our earth must, like light, move through the ether. Thus light travelling in the same direction as the earth would travel more slowly relative to us, and light in the reverse direction faster, than light travelling in a direction perpendicular to, and therefore unaffected by, the earth's motion. It follows that light would take slightly longer to travel to and fro through a fixed distance along the earth's direction of motion than to travel similarly in a direction perpendicular to this—and for the same reason that an aircraft takes slightly longer to cover a ground distance of 200 miles upwind and back again than to fly 400 miles in still air.[1] Using two mirror-pairs each 22 metres apart, Michelson and Morley had devised a delicate optical apparatus well able to measure the tiny anticipated time difference. They carried out a long series of experiments in 1881; these were repeated in 1887, and again by Morley and Miller in 1904, each series being more accurate than before. These experiments are famous precisely because no time difference was observed. This posed the most difficult problem confronting physicists, among whom Einstein saw clearly that the various explanations offered were all highly unsatisfactory.

However, Einstein's first involvement with the nature of light concerned other issues. Planck had recently published his controversial theory that radiation is emitted in tiny, indivisible packets or 'quanta'. Planck had confined his 'quantum theory' to the case of black body radiation, that is radiation from a hot body which is not hot enough to emit visible radiation. But Einstein envisaged that Planck's theory must apply to all forms of radiation, including light. So he asserted that light comprises a stream of tiny packets of energy—'light quanta' or 'photons'—which stay close together and propagate *as a beam,* yet possess *some wave-like properties.* Thus, Einstein gave birth to the concept now often referred to as 'the dual nature of light'. This is now a familiar concept in both scientific and philosophical circles, but it required courage for a young man to make any such assertion in 1905.

Einstein applied his theory to the results obtained during early experimental work on the circumstances under which a photoelectrically sensitive surface emits

[1] If the plane's speed is 500 m.p.h. and the wind's is 100 m.p.h., the round trip takes 30+20=50 minutes, as compared with 48 minutes in still air.

electrons when light strikes it. One aspect of these results was inexplicable on any wave theory of light, but Einstein's calculations showed that his 'photon' theory required just this sort of result. Indeed his calculations were far more precise than the early experiments: accurate experimental confirmation of his calculations was obtained later by Millikan. Einstein's paper formed part of the background work leading eventually to the photoelectric cell, and to television. In 1922, when his general theory of relativity was famous but controversial, Einstein was awarded the Nobel Prize at least nominally for his work on the photoelectric effect.

Einstein's early work , mostly published in the Leipzig journal, *Annalen der Physik*, shows very clearly both his entirely theoretical manner of working and his broad, imaginative grasp of many facets of physics. His immense industry is apparent in that his papers on Brownian motion and on the photoelectric effect, and his epoch-making paper on the special theory of relativity, all appeared in the same year, 1905, and indeed in the same volume, 17, of the *Annalen*.

The Special Theory of Relativity

Initial assumptions

'Special relativity' grew from Einstein's belief that the conclusion to be drawn from the Michelson-Morley experiments is that the velocity of light does not vary, however the observer may be moving; it became a major scientific theory when Einstein saw that conclusion as simply one case of a far more general assumption. This assumption is hinted at—and no more—in the deceptively straightforward title of the 1905 paper in which Einstein expounds his theory. The title is 'On the Electrodynamics of Moving Bodies'. The assumption is that the laws not only of mechanics but also of electrodynamics, of optics, and of all physical phenomena, are invariant, that is to say are the same, with respect to *all* co-ordinate systems that are moving *uniformly* relative to one another (and not subject to either acceleration or rotation).

Those familiar with elementary co-ordinate geometry should omit all but the final sentence of this present paragraph, but the notion of a 'co-ordinate system' may be unfamiliar to some readers. There are, however, two instances of a co-ordinate system in everyday use, though without this term being used. The marks on a ruler form a one-dimensional co-ordinate system, denoting the distances or 'co-ordinates' of points on the ruler's edge from the zero mark. Again, the east-west and north-south lines printed on a large-scale map form a two-dimensional co-ordinate system in which we can conveniently give map references in terms of distances or co-ordinates first eastwards and then northwards from some datum point. In mathematics this datum point is called the origin, and is usually denoted by the letter O. For measurements in space we require a three-dimensional (hereafter termed a 3–*d*) co-ordinate system consisting of 3 plane surfaces meeting each other perpendicularly at the origin, O, like adjacent faces of a box. The mutually perpendicular lines in which these planes intersect—like the 3 adjacent edges of a box—are known as the 'axes'. Referred to such a co-ordinate system the positions of all points are repre-

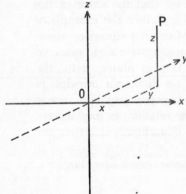

sented by three numbers, for which in general we traditionally use the letters (x, y, z). For any particular point each of these letters will have a particular value, representing the number of distance-units (feet, metres, . . .) as measured in the direction of each axis from the origin to the point (distances in the opposite

18

direction to that of the axis being counted as negative).
In order to represent *happenings* and not simply timeless
spatial positions, a fourth dimension is added to represent time; thus a 4–d co-ordinate system (x, y, z, t) has
three dimensions of space and one of time.

We can now consider Einstein's first assumption:[2]

(1) 'The laws by which the states of physical systems
undergo change are not affected, whether these changes
of state be referred to the one or the other of two co-
ordinate systems, in uniform [relative] motion'.

Einstein calls this *'the principle of relativity'*. He sharply
distinguishes it from the much more restricted assertion
that the laws of *mechanics* are unchanged when referred
to any such co-ordinate system. An obvious mechanical
instance is the law of inertia : a body subjected to no
external forces will continue in uniform motion (of which
rest is a special case) relative to *any* co-ordinate system
which is itself moving uniformly; such co-ordinate systems
are termed 'inertial systems'. Thus, passengers in a suffi-
ciently smooth-running train travelling at steady speed
along a straight, level track could in theory play billiards,
oblivious of whether the train was travelling at 80, or 40,
or 0 m.p.h. : in each case, when struck a ball would pro-
ceed in a straight line relative to the billiard-table.

As regards mechanics, this was familiar ground. But
it needed Einstein's genius to see that the scope of this
principle extends to *all* scientific 'laws'. For example, it
extends to the fact that, as Maxwell's equations show,
all electromagnetic waves propagate through space at
the same constant velocity. As said above, light also
travels at this same velocity. Thus Einstein's 'principle of
relativity' asserts that electromagnetic and light waves
travel at this particular speed relative to *any* inertial
system. It follows that waves of starlight cannot require

[2]. Both assumptions are quoted from Einstein's 1905 paper, which
is included in *The Principle of Relativity* (see Reading List).

an 'ether' in which to propagate, for their velocity would then be constant *only* with respect to the 'ether'. There is no 'ether': light and radio waves *can* travel through empty space. The Michelson-Morley experiment is now satisfactorily explained: the velocity of light is the same with respect to each mirror-pair, so obviously light takes equal times to travel to and fro between either pair.

Einstein's second assumption is:

(2) 'Every light ray moves in a "rest" co-ordinate system with the determined velocity c, whether the ray be emitted by a stationary or by a moving body.'

This further and suprising[3] assertion that light's velocity is unaffected by the velocity of the *source* emitting it was subsequently confirmed in 1913, when the Dutch astronomer De Sitter studied certain double stars. These star-pairs rotate uniformly around one another; certain pairs are so located that at times one star is moving with appreciable velocity towards us whilst its partner moves away from us. Now if, as one might expect, light travels towards the earth faster when its source is itself travelling towards us, and vice versa, then these double stars would appear to rotate round one another with varying velocity, due to the slightly varying time that their light would take to reach us. De Sitter found *no* such variation —a 'nil return' similar to that of Michelson-Morley. Hence, the velocity of light must be independent of the velocity of its source.[4]

It should be stressed that the word 'relativity' is here always used in the sense of relativity to a co-ordinate

[3] See below, pp. 21-22.

[4] Due to the 'Doppler effect' this is not the case as regards the light's *frequency*. When a light source is receding from us each successive light-wave takes a little longer to reach us, and the light's apparent frequency undergoes a 'red shift' towards the red, low-frequency, end of the spectrum. This effect is well-known with sound waves: the pitch of an express train's whistle sounds appreciably higher when the train is approaching, and lower when it is receding, than when it is stationary.

system, and thus to any observer, be he scientist or child, travelling with that system. It has nothing whatever to do with the sound doctrines that any literary or artistic work is in part relative to the period and personality of its author, and that the impression it makes is in part relative to the person studying it.

By 1905 there was considerable experimental evidence suggesting the constancy of the velocity of light; indeed an increasing number of physicists were inclined to accept this constancy, Einstein's assumption (2), and to reject the unrestricted principle of relativity (1). But Einstein, realizing that the principle of relativity undoubtedly applies throughout the realm of *mechanical* phenomena, places great emphasis upon the *philosophical* point that it is extremely improbable that a principle of such potential generality should apply to only one domain of phenomena. Einstein's procedure, therefore, is to assume that the principle of relativity applies without restriction and, as a special case of this, that the velocity of light in a vacuum is always constant. He then rigorously explores, and accepts, the consequences of these assumptions.

The core of the special theory

One consequence of Einstein's assumptions is that the normal rule for adding velocities cannot apply to light. When a fighter-bomber flies over its target firing all its guns, the velocity relative to the ground of shells from its forward-firing guns will equal the muzzle velocity *plus* the speed of the aircraft, whereas shells from rear-facing guns have a ground-velocity equal to the muzzle velocity *minus* the speed of the aircraft. But if instead of firing guns it flashes two searchlights, fore and aft, the velocity of each light beam relative to the ground is precisely *c*, irrespective of the speed of the aircraft. The speed of light is 186.000 miles per second. Let us suppose—

impractically—that the aircraft's speed is only slightly less, say 180,000 miles per second. One would expect the ground-speed of its forward searchlight-beam to be 186,000 + 180,000 m.p.s., whereas Einstein claims it to be precisely 186.000 m.p.s. Comparing these figures suggests why Einstein has been spoken of as the fellow for whom one plus one need not equal two.

But one plus one does equal two, provided that this equation's component parts are broadly similar. It follows from the above that, in some way that is very far from obvious, we must be combining dissimilar things : either fast-moving-aircraft-time and earth-time must differ so fundamentally that they cannot simply be added together, or there must be a fundamental difference as regards distance-measurements by airborne and earth-bound observers. Both differences occur; that with regard to time-measurement is the harder to grasp.

The nature of time has been one of the perennial problems discussed by philosophers. It is part of the importance of the special theory of relativity that it here forces the philosopher to learn from the physicist—forces him, in fact, to examine the nature and the *measurement* of time, as distinct from theorizing about it. And it is a major part of Einstein's own intellectual achievement that he was here willing to abandon widely-held assumptions. He always preferred calculation based on theory to 'common-sense', and therefore refused to extend the common-sense notion of 'simultaneous' to the more complex case of two spatially distant events. That this is, indeed, more complex was brought home to television viewers watching the first return of astronauts from the moon. The vital 'burn', which propels the returning module out of lunar orbit and—if all goes well—sets it heading for home, occurs on the far side of the moon, when the moon acts as a barrier interrupting radio communication. So we all wait in suspense for the module to emerge from this eclipse. As I hear the commander's voice, I glance at my watch and see that its seconds-hand coincides with the number 30. But I am aware that this does not tell me that the module's emergence from eclipse and this co-incidence of my seconds-hand with the number 30 are genuinely simultaneous events. As the announcer has explained, the capsule will in fact have emerged from eclipse $1\frac{1}{2}$ seconds earlier; our suspense has been slightly prolonged by the fact that radio waves take that time to travel between moon and earth. If there is any real simultaneity as between events in my sitting room and events near the moon it can only be a calculated simultaneity based on measurement of the time radio waves take to traverse the intervening distance.

But the constancy of the velocity of light with respect to all uniformly-moving co-ordinates systems raises still deeper problems for the concept of simultaneity. Einstein illustrates this with the thought-experiment of imagining that a long, very fast-moving train is travelling with uniform velocity along a straight embankment, and that two lightning flashes strike two points on this embankment, A and B; these two points are far apart; the train is travelling in the direction from A towards B. Einstein asks us to consider what it would mean to assert that these two flashes occurred simultaneously. He suggests the obvious definition: the two flashes can be defined as occurring simultaneously if they are seen at the same moment by an observer, O, standing on the embankment at the mid-point, M, of AB (and equipped with mirrors so that he can see both A and B at the same moment). Since light travels at the same speed in all directions it will take the same time to travel from B to M as from A to M: if the two flashes are observed at M at the same time, t_1, then they can be said to have occurred, at A and at B respectively, at the same slightly earlier time, t_0—i.e., they can be defined as 'simultaneous'. So far, be it noted, all measurements of both time and distance are relative to the co-ordinate system represented by the railway embankment.

The complication is that these same lightning flashes will not appear simultaneous to a second observer, O', similarly equipped with mirrors but travelling in the train, and positioned at the mid-point of the length $A'B'$ of the train (the coaches A', B' being those passing beside A, B when the two flashes occurred). Light from each of the two lightning flashes travels towards the train-system observer, O', with velocity c, irrespective of the velocity of the train. However, during the brief time interval it takes light to travel from B towards him, O' will himself have travelled nearer to B, thus reducing the distance this light has to travel and therefore shortening the time that flash B takes to reach him. Conversely, during this time interval O' will have moved farther from A, whose flash therefore takes a slightly longer time to reach him. Therefore two flashes which are simultaneous for observer O living in the embankment system are not simultaneous for observer O' living in the train-system, despite the fact that observers O and O' remain comparatively close together during the brief time interval in question. This state of affairs is very remarkable indeed. As we have seen, suitable calculations make it possible to extend the concept of simultaneity to cover distant events occurring within a single reference-system. But as regards events occurring in several different systems moving uniformly relative to one another there is no self-consistent concept of simultaneity: no such concept can be either observed or calculated; indeed the very existence of such a concept is impossible.

This total non-existence of any concept of simultaneity whose scope is all-embracing merits further consideration. Let us imagine two rapidly successive series of light signals A_1, A_2, A_3, . . ., B_1, B_2, B_3, . . ., emitted respectively at the spatially distant origins of two systems A, B, which are in uniform motion relative to one another. Each series —e.g., the A–signals—will be received in emission-order by all observers. But different pairs of flashes will appear simultaneous to different observers: A_4 and B_5 may appear simultaneous to one observer, A_4 and B_6 to another, and A_5 and B_4 to some third observer. Furthermore, the signals will be received in different orders by observers in widely different positions—$A_1, A_2, B_1, A_3, B_2, \ldots$, or $B_1, A_1, B_2, B_3, A_2, \ldots$, or whatever. This implies not only that there is no all-embracing concept of simultaneity but also that there is no one time-sequence valid for all uniformly-moving reference systems, and within which all the happenings in the universe occur. This discovery of the relativity of *time* to reference *system* constitutes Einstein's most original and most audacious contribution to physics, and a major contribution to natural philosophy.

The better to understand it we first note the 'classical', pre-relativity, way of transforming—of, so to say, transferring one's allegiance—from one co-ordinate system to another. This procedure is very straightforward. We consider two co-ordinate reference systems moving uniformly relative to another. The first system, S, has origin O, spatial axes Ox, Oy, Oz, and co-ordinates denoted by the letters (x, y, z, t), t being the time co-ordinate. The second system S', has origin O', spatial axes $O'x'$, etc., and co-ordinates denoted by (x', y', z', t'). For simplicity we assume that initially (when $t = t' = O$) the origins O and O' coincide, that corresponding spatial axes are parallel, and that O' moves along Ox with uniform velocity v. Then if any particular point-event (i.e., an occurrence of brief duration located at a geometrical point, such as a torch-flash) has co-ordinates $(x, y, z, t,)$ with reference to S and (x', y', z', t') with reference to S', the latter co-ordinates are given in terms of the former by these 'classical' transformation equations

$$x' = x - vt, \; y' = y, \; z' = z \qquad (1)$$
$$t' = t \qquad (2)$$

Equations (1) are geometrically obvious from the fact that, in time t, O' moves a distance vt along Ox. Equation (2) is an assumption, the pre-relativity assumption that all events, wherever and in whatever reference system they occur, take place within one single time sequence.

However, Maxwell's immensely important equations for electromagnetic fields are not what mathematicians call 'invariant' with respect to the above transformation equations: that is to say, they do not retain the same underlying form when a transformation is made from one such co-ordinate system to another. Prior to Einstein, the distinguished physicist H. A. Lorentz had devoted much work to examining this. He succeeded in devising a set of four variables, conveniently denoted by x', y', z' and t' and bound to the initial variables x, y, z, and t by a set of comparatively straightforward transformation equations, such that Maxwell's equations *do* remain invariant when transformed from the initial variables to this particular set of new variables. We quote these Lorentz equations because they play a major role in Einstein's special theory of relativity.

Readers with little mathematics can perfectly well skip over the actual equations, provided they note the comments which immediately follow—for not only the form but also the consequences of special relativity largely arise out of these equations, as re-interpreted by Einstein.

The transformation equations for obtaining the new variables are:

$$x' = \frac{x - vt}{\sqrt{1 - \dfrac{v^2}{c^2}}}, \qquad y' = y,\ z' = z, \qquad (3)$$

$$t' = \frac{t - \dfrac{vx}{c^2}}{\sqrt{1 - \dfrac{v^2}{c^2}}}. \qquad (4)$$

Note that for everyday purposes, when v is very small compared with the immensely high velocity of light, c, these equations do not differ appreciably from the 'classical' transformation equations.

Lorentz himself continued to accept the prevalent assumption as to the absolute nature of both space and time. Thus he did not regard his new set of variables as representing the actual co-ordinates of space and time in the second frame of reference, but rather as mathematically convenient variables facilitating certain calculations. He came somewhere near to grasping their true significance in that he used the variable t' to define a 'local time'; but it never occurred to him that this local time is in fact *the* time which a rapidly-moving observer would measure, and would live by. He also attempted to explain the Michelson-Morley result by suggesting that moving bodies, including the earth, contract along their direction of motion. Lorentz could not deduce this from his transformation equations, because he did not regard the new variables as co-ordinates. He suggested that rapid motion might increase the binding forces between adjacent molecules, and so cause contraction. But this remained a suspiciously convenient assumption, for which there was and is no evidence.

It was the genius of Albert Einstein that in 1905, when his elders were still puzzled and offering only artificial solutions of these problems, he succeeded in showing that the co-ordinates of space and time of two observers moving uniformly relative to one another 'are really interlocked by the Lorentz formulas', which express 'the relations which *physically* exist between the spatial and temporal co-ordinates of [such] observers. A daring hypothesis indeed, before which the perspicacious mind of Lorentz recoiled!'[5] Once this is realized, certain important principles immediately follow :

[5] Quoted from de Broglie's article in *Albert Einstein: Philosopher-Scientist,* ed. P. A. Schilpp (pp. 113, 112).

(*a*) Space and time are inextricably interconnected : note how both x and t occur in each of the formulas for x' and for t'. For this reason, as Einstein's former teacher Minkowski showed in his famous 1908 paper 'Space and Time',[6] it is both philosophically correct and, for certain purposes, mathematically convenient to treat the universe and its happenings as a 4-dimensional world in which space and time are combined in the single concept of '*space-time*'.

(*b*) The x'–equation (3), above, can be rewritten as

$$x - vt = x'. \quad \sqrt{1 - \frac{v^2}{c^2}} \qquad (3,a)$$

We now consider a moving rod of length L', which belongs to the moving system S' and lies along its direction of motion. Simultaneous measurements are made of the two ends of this rod as observed from the 'stationary' S-system ; these indicate the rod's apparent length to be L. It follows from equation (3,*a*) that

$$L = L'. \quad \sqrt{1 - \frac{v^2}{c^2}}$$

(This is because these measurements give the values of x corresponding to the two ends of the rod, which lies along and moves along Ox. So its apparent length is simply the difference between the two measurements. Since these are simultaneous, the ' $- vt$ ' term remains the same and cancels out on subtraction—leaving on the left hand side of the equation the single term L, as above.)

[6] This highly mathematical paper is in *The Principle of Relativity* (see Reading List).

Note that the rod moves with and forms part of system S′, so that L′ is its actual length—whereas L is its apparent length as measured from another system. On Einstein's theory it is not the rod itself that contracts, but measurements of the rod's length made in other co-ordinate systems. (Since $y′=y$, $z′=z$, lengths perpendicular to the direction of motion are the same in either system.)

(c) To compare time-intervals in the two systems we consider two clocks (e.g., atomic clocks) situated, and remaining, at the origins O, O′ of the two systems. To simplify the algebra required, we consider in this instance how an observer in system S′ would measure a time-interval or atomic pulse of the S clock whose duration, as measured by the S–clock itself, is T. Since this clock remains at O, x is always zero. So equation (4), above, becomes simply

$$t′ = t \cdot \frac{1}{\sqrt{1 - \dfrac{v^2}{c^2}}}$$

Since this holds for all corresponding values of $t′$ and t, corresponding time-intervals satisfy the equation

$$T′ = T \cdot \frac{1}{\sqrt{1 - \dfrac{v^2}{c^2}}}$$

where T is the actual duration of the S–clock's pulse and T′ is that pulse's apparent duration as measured from the other, S′, system. The inequality of T′ and T shows that time does not pass equably and uniformly throughout the universe—its rate of passing varies from one moving system to another. Now $\dfrac{1}{\sqrt{1 - \dfrac{v^2}{c^2}}}$ will be greater than 1,

29

since $\sqrt[\cdot]{1 - \dfrac{v^2}{c^2}}$ is less than 1. Thus time-durations oc-

curring in fast-moving systems appear greater, or dilated, when measured from other systems. This is known as 'time dilation'; it is the most puzzling and the most disputed feature of special relativity, and is further discussed below.

(*d*). Einstein's special theory leaves everyday mechanics unaffected, but does affect the mechanics—the mass and energy—of any fast-moving body or particle whose velocity is not small compared with the velocity of light. Einstein obtained a new formula for the kinetic energy (or movement-energy) of such bodies, from which it follows that their effective mass increases as their velocity increases.[7] He also proved that if a body gives out in radiation an amount of energy E, its mass, m, diminishes by the tiny amount $\dfrac{E}{c^2}$; (c, the velocity of light, is a very large number). Einstein suggested in 1905 that this might be tested 'with bodies whose energy-content is variable to a high degree (e.g. with radium salts)'; he did not then consider the converse relationship, expressed by the now famous equation $E = mc^2$, which shows that an immensely large amount of energy would be released if part of the mass of a substance could be converted into energy. It was many years before the practicability of this was established.

It occurs in two nuclear processes. Nuclear reactors and the original atomic (A–) bomb use nuclear fission, the splitting of 'uranium–235' atoms into parts whose total mass is slightly smaller than the original 'atomic weight' (235): the 'missing' mass is converted into energy. The

[7] Readers who wish to follow the mathematics should consult any technical exposition, e.g. Born's. See our Reading List.

hydrogen bomb uses nuclear fusion, whereby at very high temperatures (achieved by triggering-off with an A–bomb) hydrogen nuclei can fuse together in fours, each four forming a helium nucleus of slightly *smaller* mass than the original hydrogen nuclei. A broadly similar process of nuclear fusion provides the immense amounts of energy emitted by the sun and other stars.

As a physicist, Einstein's part in all this was confined to his initial calculation of the interrelationship, and theoretical interconvertibility, of energy and mass. His later actions on this issue as a public figure were described in chapter one. We add two further comments. On the philosophical level, special relativity bids us think in terms of a single entity, 'mass-energy', much as it also suggests the single concept, 'space-time'. As regards practical physics, the mass-increase of fast-moving electrons predicted by Einstein's theory is now a well-attested fact in daily use in modern physics laboratories, and is indeed a key factor in the design of a large amount of expensive laboratory equipment. This shows that Einstein's special theory is now a generally accepted part of modern physics—rather more widely accepted than is his general theory.

Einstein's expression for the kinetic energy of a fast-moving body shows that this energy would be infinitely great if the body's velocity equalled that of light. (The factor $\dfrac{1}{\sqrt{1 - \dfrac{v^2}{c^2}}}$ occurs in this formula, and if $v = c$ this factor becomes infinite, since its denominator (bottom) is zero.) It follows that no material particle can attain the velocity of light. Furthermore, nothing can travel faster than light. (This same factor occurs repeatedly in the above formulae; a negative number has no real square root; v cannot exceed c.) Some philosophers dislike the arbitrariness of a maximal velocity. But the experimental confirmation of special relativity shows that any such dislike must be overcome.

Time dilation, and the 'clock paradox'

Two important experimental results support the concept of time dilation. We earlier noted the 'Doppler effect', whereby the apparent frequency of an energy emission increases if the source moves towards the observer. Motion in a direction perpendicular to the observer's line-of-sight has no such effect: as the express's engine flashes past one hears the true note of its whistle; if such motion does slow down the apparent frequency, this can only be due to time dilation, the slowing-down of the apparent rate at which time elapses at and for the fast-moving energy-source. Einstein suggested in 1907 the possibility of confirming time dilation by measuring the frequency of the light emitted from a beam of particles which are moving fast across the line of vision, and comparing this with the standard frequency of similar light emissions. Thirty-one years later Ives and Stilwell achieved sufficient accuracy for this purpose. Their important experiments, too complicated to describe here, provide quantitative confirmation of the time dilation calculations integral to Einstein's special theory of relativity. (Similar but even more accurate experiments have recently provided closer confirmation.)

Less precise but more fascinating support comes from a species of transient radioactive particle known as mu-mesons. ('Mesons' comprise a whole range of such particles, different types being distinguished by various Greek letters: 'mu' corresponds to our 'm'.) These particles form part of the fall-out produced as cosmic rays strike our earth's outer atmosphere and collide with its nuclei. Showers of particles are emitted from these collisions: some of these showers travel downwards to the earth's surface, where they are found to contain a variety of particles, including mu-mesons. The latter have also been produced and studied in laboratories, from which it has been ascertained that the average 'proper lifetime' of a mu-meson, from formation to decay, is some two microseconds, that is two-millionths of a second. (By 'proper' is meant the time-span as measured by a 'clock' travelling with the fast-moving meson; this life-span is unimaginably brief, but that of a pi-meson is some 40 times shorter.) In 2 microseconds light travels 600 metres—but the collisions between cosmic rays and upper atmosphere occur at heights of over 6,000 metres.

This is highly remarkable: it is widely agreed that nothing travels faster than light, yet these mesons travel some 10 times farther than would appear possible. However, it has been estimated that the velocity of these mu-mesons is only very slightly less that that of light, so that their time dilation factor is about 10. That these mu-mesons do reach the earth's surface is thus explained by the fact that two microseconds of *their* time corresponds to twenty of *ours,* during which a particle moving at almost the speed of light travels 6,000 metres. Time dilation may appear highly curious, as do many things in modern physics, but there is strong evidence in its support.

We now turn to the famous 'clock paradox', an argument with which some philosophers and physicists have tried to refute time dilation. Here twin brothers represent the 'clocks'. One twin, B, makes a long journey into space in a spacecraft, which we will name Bobby, supposedly capable of travelling at, let us say, the same speed as mu-mesons.[8] Bobby then stops, reverses, and

---

[8] So high a velocity is impractical for a spacecraft, but this does not affect the principle of the argument.

returns to earth at the same speed. If, when he alights after his journey, twin B is *four* years older than when he set off, he will find that his brother A, who remained on earth, is *forty* years older; B is now 36 years younger than his twin! This first part of the argument is largely emotive: the unequal ageing of two twins is indeed surprising, but we have found strong grounds for regarding it as correct: time would pass 10 times more slowly in spacecraft Bobby, as compared with earth. (We cannot here discuss whether, correspondingly, living organisms in Bobby would age more slowly: there seems every reason to suppose that they would.)

The second part of the paradox is more subtle. Einstein's special theory requires that the relationship between the measurements of distance and of time-duration in two relatively-moving 'inertial' co-ordinate systems is a symmetrical relationship. Either of the two systems can be taken as datum, and the other system as moving relative to it. One could regard spacecraft Bobby as at rest and the earth as moving rapidly away from it, reversing, and returning. Either description, it is claimed, is equally permissible—but according to the second description it is earth-time which is dilated as compared with Bobby-time, and twin A returns younger than B. Since two persons cannot each be younger than the other, a logical contradiction is asserted.

This part of the 'paradox' is fallacious. The relationship between the earth and the spacecraft is not a symmetrical relationship—such as X being a brother of Y—because one cannot ignore their very different situations relative to the universe as a whole: the earth orbits slowly round its sun, whereas the spacecraft hurtles far out into space and back again. If there were two spacecraft, B and C, making similar journeys but in opposite directions, then the relationship between these would be symmetrical, and occupants of both crafts

34

would age over the journey by 4 years whilst earthbound friends aged by 40 years.

Furthermore, Bobby accelerates and decelerates twice and so does not comprise an 'inertial' system (neither, strictly, does the earth). The time spent in accelerating may be short compared with the long journey at steady speed, but if we wish to regard Bobby as at rest, then we must consider it as at rest in a system subject to acceleration, and as such governed not by the special but by the general theory of relativity. Using that theory we find that, whichever system we take as our datum, the twin in Bobby ages less than the twin on earth. The 'clock paradox' argument is fallacious; time dilation may be curious, but it is a feature of the universe.

The Search to Generalize Relativity

New problems

The originality and independence of Einstein's thinking are forcefully seen in the special theory of relativity of 1905; but his subsequent generalizing of that theory constitutes his greatest intellectual feat. His general theory of relativity was published first in 1915 and then, in final form, in 1916. As compared with special relativity, Einstein's general theory uses very advanced mathematics which only the specialist can understand; some of its practical applications are, however, much easier to grasp than those of special relativity—which explains why it was the *general* theory that made Einstein world famous.

Einstein's special theory has two artificial limitations: it is restricted to systems moving relative to one another with uniform velocity in a straight line, thus excluding acceleration, rotation, and motion along a curved path; and it is inapplicable to the gravitational forces which

35

are so fundamental a feature of the universe. Thus in searching for a more general form of relativity theory he was primarily concerned with two things, *acceleration* and *gravitation* : this perhaps helped him to see a fundamental principle of nature where others saw only the coincidence that, neglecting air resistance, all bodies accelerate at the same rate in a given gravitational field. (Thus, when dropped by an astronaut, feather and golf ball fell together on to the moon's surface.) Einstein saw in this '*the principle of equivalence*' whereby the effects of gravitation and of accelerated motion are *in principle equivalent and indistinguishable*.

Einstein deduced this principle from one of his famous 'thought experiments'. Imagine a gigantic skyscraper containing a lift (or elevator) which has been allowed to fall freely under gravity. Half a century before astronauts began getting into orbit, Einstein envisaged the now-familiar condition of weightlessness that would appertain in such a lift : the effects of gravity and of the corresponding acceleration cancel each other out so that to those in the lift there appears to be no gravitational force acting, and they are unaware of their acceleration. Again, when any express lift slows down an occupant feels heavier, in that the pressure of the floor on his feet increases, and any suitcase he is carrying also feels heavier. He assumes that the lift is decelerating—but his feelings are precisely the same as those he would experience if the earth's gravitational pull suddenly (and hypothetically) increased.

Einstein soon applied this principle to the problem of the effect of a gravitational field upon a beam of light. By the principle of equivalence this effect will be the same as that produced by accelerating the light-source, an effect which is easily deduced from his hypothetical free-falling lift. We now suppose lift, lift-shaft and skyscraper to be made of glass, and a car headlamp to be fastened to one wall of the lift and beamed horizontally towards the opposite wall. Now a free-falling lift in which the effects of acceleration and of gravity cancel each other out is tantamount to an 'inertial system', in which light travels in a straight line with constant velocity c. Relative to an observer on the ground, therefore, the light beam has *constant horizontal velocity*, together with *constant downward acceleration*. Now precisely this combination applies when a stone is thrown horizontally from the top of a cliff : the stone's path is curved, and although its horizontal velocity is constant (neglecting air resistance) its total velocity increases due to its downward acceleration. Similarly, when light travels through a gravitational field its path is very slightly curved—only slightly, because its velocity so vastly exceeds that of a stone (or a bullet); as we have seen, this bending is measurable in the case of starlight passing through the intense gravitational field close to the sun. Also, the velocity of light is no longer strictly constant when gravitation (or acceleration) is taken into account.

Einstein's principal goal in the period 1908–1916 was to establish a set of field equations enabling one to calculate the *gravitational field*—that is, the size and direction of the gravitational pull—at any point in, for example, the space extending out around the sun, and then to find the *equations of motion* for bodies moving freely in this field. The general theory of relativity is the theory by means of which these sets of equations can be obtained in particular cases. Indeed, it is often referred to as Einstein's theory of gravitation. Einstein soon saw that when one generalizes out from special relativity, whilst still assuming that the special theory is valid in most limited regions of space, one is inevitably involved in using non-Euclidean geometry.

This is seen by considering a rotating disc—one of the

simplest forms of motion, other than the uniform motion in a straight line to which the special theory is confined. If, when stationary, 100 measuring rods make up the length of the disc's diameter, then $100\pi = $ approx. 314 rods are needed to place around its circumference. When rotating rapidly, however, the rods along a diameter are unaltered in length, being perpendicular to the direction of motion, whereas those fastened around the circumference are contracted by virtue of their motion so that more than 314 rods would be needed: thus Euclid's theorem that the circumference of any circle is π times longer than its diameter does not hold for fast-rotating discs. Now as rotation produces an acceleration towards the centre,[9] it is equivalent to a gravitational field. So we have here a particular instance of the general fact that wherever there is a gravitational field the geometry of our world is not, strictly speaking, Euclidean (although it will for all normal purposes appear to be so). This is discussed below. We here add only that Euclid's geometry consists of a tightly interlocking system of theorems, all of which are logically necessary consequences of its basic assumptions. Thus, the invalidity of just one of these theorems shows that Euclid's geometry is fundamentally, and not just slightly, inapplicable to the region in question.

Einstein's special theory shows space and time to be inextricably interlocked, so that its geometry is inevitably four-dimensional. The *special* theory can use the 4–*d* equivalent of the familiar geometry of Euclid. But, as we have seen, general relativity requires a non-Euclidean geometry. One cannot understand how Einstein achieved

[9] Hence the confusing term 'centrifugal force'. A cyclist leans inwards when taking a bend fast, so as to produce an inwards (or 'centripetal') force capable of supplying the necessary acceleration towards the geometrical centre of the bend. Entering the bend fast without this acceleration would cause him to crash outwards: 'centrifugal force' would make him a centre-fugitive.

his general theory without some consideration of its geometry. We therefore discuss the fundamental properties of this geometry, avoiding its advanced mathematics. We later discuss the philosophical question, 'How can geometry be non-Euclidean?'

The geometry used by Einstein

Einstein's general theory uses, and further develops, the two-dimensional geometry of curved surfaces developed by Gauss, and extended to three- and four-dimensional space by his pupil, Riemann. Gauss examined the intrinsic geometry of curved surfaces, that is to say the geometry that would be experienced by an ant who only crawls over the surface and knows nothing of the wider world. Now on a *curved* surface there may be no *straight* lines, only curved lines following the contours of the surface. Euclid's geometry cannot apply on any curved surface. As an example of this, consider an ant crawling on a child's globe, and travelling a quarter of the way round its Equator, then directly North to the Pole, then directly back to its starting point. Its path is the equivalent, on a spherical surface, to a triangle. But whereas the angles of Euclid's triangles add up to two right angles, all three angles of this triangle are right angles.

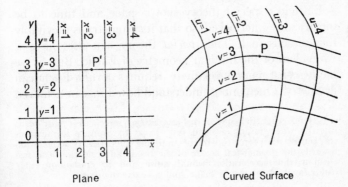

Plane   Curved Surface

The traditional, so-called Cartesian, co-ordinates (x, y) formed by pairs of perpendicular straight lines cannot be used. But Gauss saw that any curved surface can be completely mapped by any suitable 'net' of curves comprising two sets of curves, labelled u and v. The members of each set never intersect one another, but they intersect all the members of the other set. Consecutive curves in each set are numbered 1, 2, 3 . . ., and the area between each can be sub-divided as required. Thus the curved surface is completely mapped, analogously to the mapping of a plane.

The basic constituent of a curved surface is the *line element*; indeed the shape of any small region of a surface is determined by all the small movements—called line elements—that can be made outwards along the surface, in various directions, from a point P in the middle of the region. We here use the standard notation[10] whereby dx, dy denote small changes in the values of the Cartesian co-ordinates near the point P' on the plane, and du, dv small changes in the curvilinear co-ordinates near P on the surface : in each case ds represents the length of the line element corresponding to these small changes.

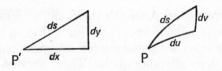

In the case of a plane, we know from Pythagoras's theorem for right-angled triangles that $(ds)^2 = (dx)^2 + (dy)^2$. In the case of a curved surface this theorem, which belongs to Euclidean geometry, does not apply, and the expression for $(ds)^2$ is more complicated : it involves $(du)^2$

[10] This notation originates in calculus, but no calculus is used in this book.

and $(dv)^2$ and also the product du, dv; and each of these terms is itself multiplied by a factor, technically known as a *coefficient,* which varies in a perfectly definite way from one point to another. (Mathematically expressed, these coefficients are functions of u and v.) These three coefficients are traditionally represented by the letter g, with suffices indicating to which co-ordinate each co-efficient relates.[11]

The values of the g's at various points on a given surface depend upon the co-ordinate system chosen, and any suitable system can be used. But there are certain fundamental properties of curved surfaces which are represented by what mathematicians call 'invariant' formulae; that is to say, whilst these formulae have to be expressed in terms of the g's, when calculated in terms of the g's corresponding to any two different co-ordinate systems the formula will always calculate out to give the same unvarying—'*invariant*'—result. The usefulness of the g's arises from this invariance, which applies to two geometrical properties that play vital roles in Einstein's general theory of relativity. We first consider these properties as they apply to curved surfaces.

(*a*) *Shortest lines.* Although there are no straight lines, there are straightest lines in the sense that on the surface there is always one path between two given points that is shorter than all other paths. These shortest lines are technically termed 'geodesics'. An example is the great circles—circles whose centre is the centre of the earth—that we use in navigation : the shortest surface route from London to New York is along a great circle. The equations of geodesics are calculable in terms of the g's, and are represented by invariant formulae.

---

[11] The length of a line element is given by the equation
$$(ds)^2 = g_{11}(du)^2 + 2g_{12}\ du.dv + g_{22}(dv)^2$$

(b) *Curvature.* The curvature of a curve or surface is a measure of the sharpness with which it bends: sharp bends have high curvature. A sphere has a surface of uniform curvature, given by curvature $=\dfrac{1}{\text{radius}}$. For other surfaces, the curvature varies from point to point; also at any given point, P, the surface may have a different curvature corresponding to every direction in which this curvature is measured. Gauss proved that the mean curvature at P can be calculated in terms of the values of the g's at P, and that this calculation yields an invariant result whatever co-ordinate system is used.

Riemann's geometry for three dimensions similarly uses three sets of curved surfaces to map a given region of space. In Euclidean space the shortest line between any two points is a straight line, and the 'curvature' of the space is zero. But where a space is non-Euclidean the shortest lines are, in general, curved. These are represented by invariant formulae analogous to the invariant formulae for geodesics on curved surfaces. Similarly, there are in 3–d invariant formulae analogous to those for the curvature of a surface. Indeed, mathematicians speak of a non-Euclidean space as being 'curved'. Since this notion that a space can be curved may appear nonsense, we add these comments: (i) Euclidean space is not curved; (ii) nobody can visualize a curved space, but modern physics has many features that can only be treated mathematically and cannot be visualized; (iii) the notion of a space being curved is entirely compatible with the fact that in it the *shortest* line between two points is in general a *curved* line.

In the case of four dimensions—which, again. one cannot visualize—space, or 'space-time', can be mapped by any suitable system of four curvilinear co-ordinates (one of which primarily represents time). The mathe-

matics is highly complicated : there are now 10 terms in
the expression for the length of a line element, and therefore, for each point in the space, 10 different g's. In
general, as in $3-d$, the shortest lines or geodesics are
curved lines, and space itself is curved. Also, both geodesics and curvature are represented by invariant formulae, which have to be calculated in terms of the 10
g's. These invariant formulae underlie Einstein's general
theory.

The general theory of relativity

Having established his starting point, namely that the
presence of gravitation entails using non-Euclidean geometry and that acceleration and gravitation are con-
nected by 'the principle of equivalence', Einstein proceeds
to make the simple but very broad assumption that 'the
principle of relativity' of his special theory remains valid
when applied not just to 'inertial systems' but to any
arbitrarily chosen Gaussian co-ordinate system : 'The
general laws of nature are to be expressed by equations
which hold good for all systems of co-ordinates . . .'.[12]

In seeking the equations of motion of a particle (or a
planet) moving freely in a gravitational field, Einstein
points out that the geodesic lines of a non-Euclidean
space correspond to the straight lines of Euclidean space,
and that according to special relativity (as also according
to Newton) a freely movable body not subject to such
external forces as gravitation moves uniformly in a
straight line. Einstein proceeds from this to the more
general assumption that a freely movable body which is
subjected to gravitational forces will always move along
a geodesic : gravitation acts as a field of force, and exerts
a curving influence in space such that bodies naturally

[12] Quotations are from Einstein's 1916 paper on the general
theory, included in *The Principle of Relativity*.

follow the path of least resistance, which is a geodesic curve. As we shall see, experimental evidence confirms this key assumption.

Now the formulae for geodesics are invariant. Therefore, having chosen any convenient co-ordinate system, and assuming that the values of the 10 g's at any point can be calculated, one can use complicated mathematical procedures to obtain equations for the shortest lines or geodesics, and therefore for the path of a particle moving freely in a gravitational field, always provided that one can calculate the 10 functions representing the 10 g's for this gravitational field.

In obtaining the equations for a gravitational field Einstein establishes that it is the presence of gravitation which makes a region's geometry non-Euclidean, and thereby causes the space in question to be 'curved'. Thus Einstein asserts that the geometry of a region of the universe *depends upon and is affected by* the disposition of matter in and near the region. We further examine this difficult notion below, noting here that it is only gravitation which thus affects the geometry : electro-magnetic fields have no corresponding effect.

Einstein confines himself to regions of space permeated by gravitation, but containing no material bodies (or electric charges). He makes a mathematically important assumption concerning one of the invariant formulae for the curvature of such a region, a formula which is equivalent to a set of 10 functions of the 10 g's : Einstein assumes that, in a region containing no matter, all 10 functions can be equated to zero. The mathematics are highly complicated, but Einstein here adopts the simplest mathematically permissible assumption. This assumption (for which, again, Einstein advances strong arguments but no rigorous proof) produces 10 equations for the 10 g's. Now, in principle, a set of 10 equations can be solved to yield specific values for each of 10 unknowns—somewhat as pupils at school solve a pair of 'simultaneous equations' and obtain values for the 2 unknowns x and y. So, having chosen the most convenient co-ordinate system, this assumption provides a method of calculating the values of the g's at each point in a gravitational field of this type. And once the g's are known, the equations of motion can also be calculated.

Einstein thus establishes the mathematical basis for his general theory of relativity. We now examine the main practical effects of this theory, first remarking that Einstein's equations are so complicated that in over fifty years solutions have been obtained for only a few comparatively straightforward problems. Fortunately these include the motion of planets, and the passage of a light-ray near the sun; both cases were worked out by Einstein himself, and both have been checked by astronomical observations.

Experimental evidence

Einstein's 1916 paper examines the special case of the gravitational field surrounding a point-mass. This field has the great simplicity and symmetry of being spherical; furthermore, for Einstein's purposes the sun can be treated as if its mass were all concentrated at its centre-point. Using his assumption concerning the curvature formula, he obtains approximate formulae (accurate to the second order of approximation) for this gravitational field. These formulae give the values of the g's at any point in this field, and this enables Einstein also to calculate the equations of motion.

Einstein suggests three ways in which his formulae could be tested experimentally. He calculates that a ray of starlight which grazes the edge of the sun bends, due to the sun's gravitational field, through a very small angle of 1.7 seconds of arc. (Each degree of an angle is subdivided into minutes and seconds like an hour, and there are 90 degrees to a right angle; so this tiny angle is approximately five-millionths of a right angle.) Due to this bending, the star's apparent position in the sky differs slightly from its true position. (Similarly, though the physical causes of the bending of light in the two cases are quite different, the apparent position of an under-water object differs from its actual position.) Einstein suggested that his calculation could be checked by com-paring, during an eclipse, the apparent position of a star that is almost in line with the sun with the position of that same star at night.

Calculations from photographs taken during the eclipse of May 29, 1919 apparently confirmed Einstein's figure for this bending and, as we have seen, made Einstein world famous. Two sets of observations were taken during that eclipse, one set at Sobral, Brazil, and the other on the West African island of Principe. The angles of bending obtained were 1.98 seconds of arc at Sobral and 1.6 seconds at Principe—the average of these two being surprisingly close to Einstein's figure, in view of the ex-treme smallness of the angle. However, some recent observations give a figure about ten per cent higher than Einstein's—as did the Sobral observations. Ironically, experimental results of the type that made Einstein famous are now regarded by some physicists as giving only somewhat doubtful support to Einstein's general theory.

Stronger confirmation of Einstein's theory has recently been obtained by measuring the effect of a gravitational field upon the rate at which 'clocks' run—i.e., in practice, the frequency of certain forms of radiation. Einstein here saw little chance of early experimental confirmation and confined himself to giving a formula for the extent to which a 'clock goes more slowly' in a gravitational field, commenting that for this reason the light from a star undergoes a 'red shift' towards the red, low frequency, end of the spectrum. This 'Einstein shift' is small, and is often combined with a Doppler effect. Nevertheless, observations of light from the sun, and from the heavy star B Sirius, provide some support for Einstein's formula. The strongest confirmation comes, however, from terrestrial experiments carried out in 1960. R. L. Mossbauer had discovered how to control certain atomic nuclei so that they emit gamma-rays with an exceedingly constant frequency, and such that minute changes in this frequency can be measured. His discovery made it possible to measure the frequency-change resulting from the tiny decrease in the strength of the earth's gravitational field corresponding to an increase in altitude of 22 metres. This measurement agreed very closely indeed with the figure as calculated from Einstein's formula.

The recent experiment of carrying atomic clocks around the world in jet aircraft and comparing these with similar clocks on the ground provides mild confirmation of both time dilation and the Einstein shift. However, the agreement between calculations and results is not impressive.

Accurate prediction of previously unknown phenomena is more exciting than accounting for facts that are well known but unexplained. Nevertheless, one of the strongest experimental supports for Einstein's general theory is the one which he calculated in detail in 1915; his theory explains and accurately accounts for a divergence between the observed motion of the planet Mercury and its calculated motion on the basis of Newton's law of gravity. According to Newton's law, a single planet would orbit the sun in an elliptical path, always remaining in the same plane. The gravitational influence of the other planets, all much less massive than the sun, will slightly deflect Mercury's path out of its original plane. Newton-based calculations show that due to the other planets the plane of Mercury's orbit should rotate very slowly through an angle of 531 seconds per century. (Accurate astronomical observations go back for very many years, so it is permissible to consider the rotation per century.) In fact, the *observed* rotation is 574 seconds per century—an excess of 43 seconds over the calculated figure.

Now Einstein's formulae for the motion around the sun of a single planet show that (disregarding the effects of the other planets) its orbit will not remain precisely in one plane, but will slightly rotate; in the case of Mercury, Einstein calculated this angle of rotation to be 43.03 seconds per century—precisely the excess rotation that had been observed, but not explained. Mercury is the planet nearest to the sun and so travels through a stronger gravitational field than the others. The next nearest planet, Venus, also confirms Einstein's theory, bearing in mind that it moves in a weaker gravitational field and the rotation of its orbit is smaller, so that both observation and calculation are less accurate than for Mercury. The unexplained element in the observed rotation of Venus's orbit is 8.4 seconds of arc per century, whilst Einstein's theory gives a rotation of 8.63 seconds per century. As regards this previously mysterious feature of planetary motion, theory and observation agree extremely closely.

The standing of Einstein's general theory

Taken together, the various items of experimental evidence offer strong and impressive confirmation of Einstein's general theory of relativity, which is now fairly generally accepted. However, this confirmation is not yet conclusive, the total quantity of relevant experimental evidence being much smaller than in the case of the special theory.

But the primary strength of the general theory of relativity derives from the inner consistency of the theory and the philosophical soundness of its basic assumptions.

Its philosophical acceptability has been attacked mainly by alleging that it is improper to make the geometry of a region, and of the universe, dependent upon the distribution of matter therein. This procedure is certainly quite contrary to our normal thinking, and was strongly denounced by the philosopher–mathematician A. N. Whitehead. But let us look carefully at what the general theory asserts. Firstly, it argues outwards, so to say, from special relativity to the conclusion that regions where there is gravitation and acceleration cannot possess a strictly Euclidean geometry, since measurements made in such a region conflict with a basic theorem of Euclid's. Secondly, Einstein regards the (non-Euclidean) geometry of a region as describing *how bodies move*—that is, as describing the paths along which freely moving bodies, and light beams, travel. This is a different concept of geometry from the one we normally employ: we think of geometry primarily as describing properties and interrelationships of static figures composed mainly of straight lines, and secondarily as applying to those features of the world that can be described by such figures. Now in physics a straight line is the path followed by a moving body subject to no external forces and to no gravitational field. Under these circumstances Einstein's *special* theory applies, and the geometry is Euclidean. The general theory of relativity simply does not apply to those regions where our normal, Euclidean geometry does accurately describe the way things move. The common accusation that Einstein allows matter to affect, and distort, geometry tends to confuse two senses in which the word 'geometry' can be used. It is only in Einstein's important but unfamiliar sense and usage of that word that matter affects geometry: it is, after all, scarcely surprising that the nature of a particular gravitational field should affect the way bodies move in that field.

Alternatively, one may wish to stress that geometry is

a purely *theoretical* study of properties of straight lines, circles, etc. Again, Einstein's theory merely points out that this theoretical, Euclidean, geometry does not strictly apply to the way things move in a world that includes gravitation. For everyday purposes Euclid's geometry certainly appears to apply to our world. But there is no sound philosophical reason for assuming that the same geometry does in fact apply both to the way things move in the world and to the theoretical figures with which Euclid's theorems are concerned.

Finally, we would emphasize the impressiveness of both the *breadth of application* and the *underlying unity* of Einstein's general theory. Newton postulated his laws of motion—his dynamics—quite separately from his law of gravitation : one of these could be correct and the other false. As first propounded, Einstein's theory also rests on two quite separate assumptions : the law of motion, along geodesics; and the highly mathematical assumption which yields the requisite equations for a straightforward gravitational field. Einstein and others came to suspect that the equations for a gravitational field in fact determine not only the strength of that field at each point but also the laws of motion within it. This was established in a 1938 paper by Einstein, Infeld and Hoffmann. Thus what began as a theory of gravitation is also a system of dynamics—a quite remarkable breadth of application.

Einstein's Later Work

Einstein did a fair amount of new, detailed work on relativity after 1916, besides that leading to the 1938 paper. He also explained it in book form (see Reading List). His general theory deals with the interrelationships between gravitation, space and time, and dynamics : it does not indicate how gravitation propagates itself. Newton supposed that the gravitational force exerted by one body on another distant body acts instantaneously. Einstein disbelieved this, and did much work searching for equations that would throw light on the problem. In 1937 he and Rosen obtained some exact solutions of the equations for a gravitational field: these solutions have significant wave-like properties (not apparent in the approximate solutions of 1916), which strongly suggests that gravitation propagates outwards in a similar manner to electromagnetic waves. Since Einstein's death, other wave-like solutions have been obtained.

But the most fascinating post-1916 development of relativity is its application to cosmology, the structure of the universe. Einstein was interested in the present structure of the universe, but not in the more speculative problems as to its origin in the remote past. Asked to comment as between two such speculations, he once replied tersely 'I was not present'. Einstein's important contribution was to show that the property of space-curvature which the general theory propounds can be developed to yield the doctrine that *space as a whole* is non-Euclidean, *finite, yet without boundaries*. This doctrine assumes that the total number of stars is finite (though immense), and that space *curves in on itself,* in the sense that a light-ray (or some hypothetical space-craft) will be gradually but continually bent round under the gravitational attraction of the entire finite universe so that if it travelled for long enough it could complete a closed curve, always curving around the centre of gravity of the universe, and return whence it originated. Einstein's initial work on this assumed a universe of constant size; but his cosmology has also been developed to comply with the now widely held view that the universe is expanding. It is much easier to think of a surface curving in on itself than of space doing this. And the case of a soap bubble, or a child's

51

balloon, suggests that Einstein's notion is basically un-affected by whether the universe be static in size or expanding : while it expands the bubble's surface remains finite, without boundary, and curving in on itself.

This notion of space bending in on itself may seem obscure, but it avoids some grave difficulties. Few physi-cists or philosophers have favoured the notion that the number of stars is infinite—philosophical difficulties apart, if there were a limitless infinity of stars one would expect the night sky to be, if not infinitely bright, at least much brighter than it is. And if the number of stars be finite, then it is at the least difficult to attach meaning to the notion of a straight line going on and on, beyond all the stars, through infinite empty space. Indeed the notion of 'empty space beyond all the stars' makes sense only on an 'absolute' theory of space. If, with most (though not all) contemporary philosophers, one regards space—and space-time—as relative to the bodies that make up the universe, then one has to deny the meaning-fulness of this notion of space beyond the stars. This suggests that the universe has a boundary, in connection with which the word 'beyond' is meaningless. Relati-vistic cosmology is not beset by these difficulties.

Other than relativity, Einstein's most important con-tribution to physics is undoubtably his use of statistics and his devising of new statistical techniques. We saw this in his early work. We find it again in his work on quantum physics in the years 1917-25. It is Einstein's opposition to the way quantum physics developed after 1924 that is now remembered : his very important con-tribution to the beginnings of that very development is often overlooked. In his 1917 paper on the quantum theory of radiation, he devised new statistical methods for calculating the various probabilities of transitions from one energy-state to another, transitions in which changes in the body emitting radiation comprise one complete quantum, or several quanta, of energy. The statistical evaluation of these transition probabilities has been a primary task of quantum physicists from then on ; they still largely use formulae that are, so to say, the children or grandchildren of those 1917 equations.

But Einstein always refused to accept the more fundamental sense in which statistics has been used in post-1924 quantum physics. According to Heisenberg's famous 'principle of indeterminacy' either the position or the momentum[13] of an electron (or similar particle) can be measured, but not both. This is also known as 'the uncertainty principle', a term which suggests what is now only a minority view, namely that this uncertainty is confined to our ability to perform measurements relating to individual particles. But the great majority of physicists hold that there is a physical indeterminacy as to the positions and velocities of individual particles because, in microphysics, the causal laws themselves are statistical in character and do not govern the precise movements of individual particles. Einstein's deep-seated opposition to this admittedly difficult notion is summed up in his famous phrase, 'God does not play at dice'.

He had already begun seeking for a *unified field theory*. His own equations for a gravitational field are different in form from Maxwell's equations for an electromagnetic field. Einstein disliked this duality of formulae; he believed that there must be a single set of equations which would represent both types of field. He equally disliked using different mathematical approaches for fields and for particles. Believing the field concept to be fundamental, he held that the mathematics of a unified field theory could also represent the presence of particles. At first, Einstein was not the only major physicist seeking some such unified theory. But as the years went by more

13 In mechanics 'momentum' denotes the product mass multiplied by velocity.

and more physicists came to see an essentially-statistical quantum theory as a distinct branch of physics; they rejected the notion of a theory whose scope would include both particles and fields; and they saw no likelihood of finding a single set of equations to represent all types of field. Sadly, therefore, Einstein became increasingly remote from most of his fellow physicists. The general view today is that seeking a unified field theory is an abortive undertaking. There are, however, a few physicists who take the view that Einstein was simply ahead of his time; new species of elementary particles, and new forces within the atom, have since been discovered, rendering his data incomplete—as ours still are. Furthermore, Einstein's 1938 paper shows that a single set of equations can have a very wide breadth of application. It seems unlikely, but it is possible that a unified field theory will be obtained by some future physicist; if so, his name will rank with those of Newton and Einstein.

3

SIGNIFICANCE

IN ASSESSING the significance of Albert Einstein, we first look briefly at his work in international affairs. From the twenties onwards, Einstein used his fame to promote peace policies and the League of Nations, and to oppose nationalism and anti-Semitism. Einstein's was one of the important moderating voices. But it is questionable how effective his influence was upon public affairs. During 1931–2, Einstein twice spent several weeks in Oxford; the economist Sir Roy Harrod recalls that he greatly liked Einstein but when 'probing him on political matters, I found that his views were liberal and enlightened, but not particularly deep'. However, Bertrand Russell, who got to know Einstein at Princeton in the early forties, pays this tribute : 'Of all the public figures that I have known, Einstein was the one who commanded my most whole-hearted admiration. . . . Einstein was not only a great scientist, he was a great man. He stood for peace in a world drifting towards war'.[14]

Einstein's religious views were not original. He once summarized them thus : 'I believe in Spinoza's God who reveals himself in the harmony of all that exists, not in a God who concerns himself with the fate and actions of men'. Rightly or wrongly, not many Jews or Christians can accept this. The religious significance of Einstein's

[14] Both comments were made in a series of B.B.C. talks on Einstein (ed. G. J. Whitrow, pp. 59, 90–91; see Reading List).

discoveries is another matter, and remains largely unexplored. Whilst many today assume that science has debunked religion, some theologians regard religion and science as belonging in largely watertight compartments. Others, myself among them, disagree with both viewpoints. Unlike Einstein, I believe in a God who is concerned as to our activities; and I find this belief compatible with our knowledge concerning the nature of the world. But this compatibility is not automatic : it depends upon what sort of a world one's knowledge reveals, and what sort of religious beliefs one holds. The main Christian philosophical tradition asserts, not that God is unconcerned as to what we do, but that God's essential nature and character remain, ultimately, quite unaffected by the world and its happenings. Now that Einstein has shown that the main features of the physical universe are inextricably interrelated, it is questionable whether any theology that believes God to be ultimately unaffected by the world's happenings—to be 'impassible' —can survive without at least very drastic modification. The branch of contemporary theology known as 'process theology' is one which explicitly rejects that particular doctrine ; it also has a certain philosophical affinity with relativity theory in that each regards the occurrences of certain events—or processes—at particular place-times as being the ultimate constituents of our world. Process philosophy and theology are best known in America ; they are beginning to receive more attention in Britain and elsewhere.[15]

As chapter 2 shows, Einstein's scientific work is of the very highest order. Predictions are rash, but it seems likely that future generations will continue to regard Einstein's

[15] See my *The Living God and the Modern World* (Hodder; also United Church Press, Philadelphia), and N. Pittenger, *Alfred North Whitehead* (Lutterworth Press; also John Knox Press). I discuss an alleged difficulty as between process theology and relativity physics in a forthcoming work.

genius and importance as comparable to those of Galileo and of Newton, and that Einstein will chiefly be remembered for his treatments of time and light and for his interrelating of mass first with energy and then with geometry. All of these matters are of the first importance for philosophy as well as for physics. Indeed, Einstein regarded himself as both a physicist and a philosopher. But it is significant that the solutions he offered to such philosophical problems as the nature of time and the 'boundary' of the universe came not from philosophical discussion but from the mathematical and logical approach of theoretical physics. Henceforth, in such matters, the philosopher must learn from the physicist. We have noted the main practical effects of Einstein's theories : the equation $E = mc^2$ led to the discovery of nuclear fission and fusion; and his doctrine that mass increases with velocity is central to all work on fast-moving particles.

We have stressed that Einstein was always a *theoretical* physicist who grappled with the fundamental interrelationships between basic physical concepts, and with the mathematics which expresses these relationships. The deep conviction that undergirded this lifelong grappling has an interesting affinity to his belief 'in Spinoza's God who reveals himself in the harmony of all that exists'. When lecturing in Oxford in 1933 on the subject of method in theoretical physics, Einstein says this : 'Our experience up to date justifies us in feeling sure that in Nature is actualized the ideal of mathematical simplicity'. Einstein also emphasizes his 'conviction that pure mathematical construction enables us to discover the concepts and the laws connecting them which give us the clue to the understanding of the phenomena of Nature'.

Einstein's remarkable power of prolonged concentration whilst grappling with problems of the greatest difficulty is certainly, from the personal point of view, the most striking feature of his life and work. His special theory of relativity results from some three years, and his general theory from a further eight years, of immense intellectual effort. At the present time, when many people move on restlessly from job to job—or just idly switch from one television channel to another—we do well to recall Einstein's intense, sustained, and single-minded concentration upon his main tasks. The closing words of a 1933 lecture in Glasgow stand as testimony to the prolonged work involved in his methods of theorizing. After speaking of his use of Riemann's geometry in his general theory, Einstein says: 'Once the validity of this mode of thought has been recognized, the final results appear almost simple . . . But the years of searching in the dark for a truth that one feels, but cannot express; the intense desire and the alternations of confidence and misgivings, until one breaks through to clarity and understanding, are only known to him who has himself experienced them'.

SHORT READING LIST

Some books by Einstein

Relativity: The Special and the General Theory. A popular Exposition (15th ed.,1954, Methuen, London, and Crown Publishers, New York).
This makes very extensive use of algebra but avoids advanced mathematics.
Ideas and Opinions (Crown Publishers, New York, 1954).
The principal collection of his general writings on politics, pacifism, science, and other matters.

Books about Einstein

MICHELMORE, PETER, *Einstein : Profile of the Man* (Apollo, New York, 1962; F. Muller, London, 1963).
VALLENTIN, ANTONIA, *Einstein* (London, 1954 : now out of print).
Einstein: the man and his achievement, B.B.C. Talks, edited by G. J. Whitrow (B.B.C., London, 1967).
INFELD, LEOPOLD, *Albert Einstein: his work and its influence on our world* (Scribners, New York and London, 1950).
LANCZOS, CORNELIUS, *Albert Einstein and the Cosmic World Order* (Wiley, New York, and Interscience Publishers, Chichester, 1965).
BORN, MAX, *Einstein's Theory of Relativity* (revised edition published by Dover Publications, New York, 1962). Uses advanced mathematics.

Miscellaneous

The Principle of Relativity (1923; reprinted by Dover Publications, New York, 1952). A collection of papers by Einstein and others, including his original papers on special and general relativity. Uses advanced mathematics.